RIBBLEHEAD

The Story
of the great viaduct
At Batty Moss
on the
Settle-Carlisle Railway

W. R. Mitchell MBE

Dedicated to

Tony Freschini
Resident Engineer, Ribblehead Viaduct restoration

Published by

Kingfisher Productions

Watershed Mill, Settle North Yorkshire BD24 9LR
www.railwayvideo.com

ISBN 978-0957336-75-9
Copyright W. R. Mitchell and Kingfisher Productions
Publisher, Roger Hardingham
First published March 2015

INTRODUCTION

John Ruskin, looking at Ingleborough on a windy day, wondered how the mountain managed to stand without rocking. A similar thought came into my mind as I parked my car near Ribblehead Viaduct. The car rocked. The viaduct stood firm as yet another storm from the west advanced up Chapel-le-Dale, stirring the air until the wind moaned between the high arches. It was like listening to part of the sound- track of a Bronte film.

The late Bishop Treacy, who suffered badly from Settle-Carlislitis, considered that the three greatest North Country wonders were York Minister, Hadrian's Wall and – the Settle-Carlisle railway. He occasionally rode on footplates, doubtless ducking if there was a wind roaring over Ribblehead Viaduct.

Someone described Ribblehead Viaduct as "like a Victorian cobweb stretched across the head of the dale". Seen from a distance, the graceful lines of the 24-arch viaduct give little indication of its bulk. See the viaduct reflected in a puddle on the track leading to it from near the Station Inn and the gigantic structure appears to be floating in space.

It is a different matter when you stand close by it, with the ponderous verticals of dressed limestone near at hand and a wind passing between the arches like the "wuthering" wind used on the sound track of a Bronte film. John Crossley, Engineer-in-Chief for the Midland Railway took a great interest in the design of Settle-Carlisle viaducts. Some idea of Victorian confidence is to be seen in their relative slender forms.

The Midland Railway began work on the Settle-Carlisle Railway when a sod was cut at Anley, near Settle, in the November of 1869. Constructing the line demanded the greatest engineering skill that had been shown in the land. The men who built the line had to have extreme physical endurance. Some of the workmen, employed building railways in far-off lands, found Ribblehead to be one of the wildest, windiest spots in the world. The line was opened for passenger traffic on 1 May, 1856.

Ribblehead Viaduct, an outstanding feature of the Settle-Carlisle Railway, stands on Batty Moss, thirteen miles from Settle Junction. A quarter of a mile in length, with 24 arches, it has a slight curve as it spans an area where several valleys meet under the gaze of high fells. It was originally referred to as Batty Wife Viaduct, after a fanciful local story. The prosaic title was Bridge No 66. Crossley, the Midland company's chief engineer, did not for a while make up his mind as to the number of arches that were needed. It might vary between eighteen and twenty-four. Crossley felt that the latter figure was desirable. It was not confirmed until the end of 1872.

A newspaper writer of 1873, reflecting on a sense of wonder left by many as Ribblehead Viaduct arose behind a "web" of wooden scaffolding, wrote: "The viaduct, when completed, will be the admiration of all lovers of imposing and massive masonry." Every sixth pier became a "king" pier, twice as thick as the others. The idea would be that if one pier fell it would take only five other piers with it. No doubt generations unborn would look upon the viaduct with wonder. They would think how clever had been their forefathers when rearing such a structure.

Ribblehead Viaduct could be a nightmare in a westerly gale. I heard from a fireman that the old Class 4 loco had not got much of a cab. "If the wind was strong, you got your fire prepared before you got on to the viaduct, and then you and your driver got tucked away in a corner and let the engine chuff across. Three motor cars were blown off a special train at the end of Blea Moor loop.

Gales had been known to stop trains as they left Ribblehead station and moved towards the viaduct, on either side of which are high, steep embankments. Scores of wagon sheets have been torn from their places and blown across country, a windfall in a literal sense for the Dales farmers.

Wagon sheets were large and heavy. A man stood near the viaduct in wild weather when he saw a sheet blow off a wagon. Said he: "That sheet floated away on the wind like a piece of confetti. It was going upwards, not downwards. I kept thinking – if that lands on a passing car, the driver won't see daylight again for ages. I have been told the highly improbable story of a man who was standing on the viaduct when the wind caught his hat, blew it under an arch, up the other side and plopped it back on his head!

Geoff Bounds, project manager when Ribblehead Viaduct was extensively renovated, described the railway as having "an almost indefinable magic – a cocktail mix of fact and folklore, acquired in over a hundred years of operations." Dealing with the restoration, day by day, was Tony Freschini, the most northerly resident engineer of the London Midland Region. Tony greatly admired the work of Victorian railway engineers.

The viaduct, built of local "black limestone", and exposed to gales from the west, is scheduled as an Ancient Monument – a monument, indeed, that is still in daily use! An engineer remarked: "You have to take your hat off to the men who built Ribblehead Viaduct. When you consider their primitive equipment, it's a fantastic piece of engineering work."

W. R. Mitchell MBE

A Glorious Setting

Ribblehead Viaduct was set amid lonely moors and fells. The fells include Ingleborough, Whernside and Blea Moor. Westerly gales, which roar up the Lune Valley and Chapel-le-Dale, batter the masonry but it stands without shuddering. There is a glorious attendance at nesting time of curlews and lapwings. The rumbling and occasional tooting of passing trains seems to blend in with nature's sounds.

When Bishop Treacy began to explore the country north of Skipton, he was thrilled by what he was to describe as "the most marvellous railway". To him it seemed as much at home as the rocks and rivers.

A railway guard with whom I chatted mentioned the occasional harsh weather. He had seen cars blown over the viaduct side in a terrific shower of sparks. When the train got to Dent box, the signalman shouted:

"Lads! Three of them Humber Snipes is missing! "And by heck, they were. We found them at first light – just scrap metal down in the stream bed."

In recent times, when the track over the viaduct were temporarily removed to allow waterproofing of the structure to take place, the weather was at its Pennine worst with howling wind and lashing rain. This did not stop the work in hand. I observed through mist and rain a locomotive with attendant crane from which a section of track was suspended as it was moved back into place.

The weather was calm when, with permission, and in the company of my old friend Peter Fox, I ascended ladders and walked on scaffolding, watching men who were skilfully engaged in restoration work. As late evening was nigh Ingleborough was empurpled and the western sky glowed red. The viaduct lay under a blaze of arc lights as the restoration work continued through the night.

A beautiful sunny day at Ribblehead. A modern diesel Sprinter unit crosses over the 24-arched viaduct with the Yorkshire peak of Pen-y-gent in the background.

The Ribblehead Landscape

Above: **The incredible landscape around Batty Moss shows the rugged, but also the idlyic setting of this part of the Settle to Carlisle line. Hundreds of years of erosion have produced the limestone landscape seen above. The whole area has one of the largest outcrops of limestone in Europe.**

Left: **The evening sunshine can produce amazing effects upon the land around the arches.**

A view from Yorkshire's highest peak Whernside. The course of the Settle-Carlisle is seen from this viewpoint some 600 meters above Ribblesdale. It illustrates to us how the architects of the railway decided on the building of a viaduct at this point. The 24 arches are clearly visible and you can see how embankments at either end were built up to meet the viaduct piers. At the top right of the photographs is the limestone quarry close to the station at Ribblehead. This is now defunct but the siding there is still very much in use, mostly for timber exporting.

One of the king piers on the viaduct. This one forms the centre of the structure and has the date embedded into one of the top stones. The close-up view gives an indication as to the vast amount of stone-work involved in the construction. In nearby Littondale, a stream was diverted to reveal the finest stone that the contractor wished for. Mr Ashwell had scoured the area to locate the very best he could find. The limestone was dug out in huge blocks weighing up to five tons each. At the quarry site, many men and a steam pump was used to dress the stone before it was conveyed to the building site by the tramway linking the two. In total, over 30,000 cubic yards of 'black' limestone was removed.

This side elevation of the viaduct shows just how big the structure is. The camera is looking west and across the snow-covered moor. This whole area was covered in activity whilst the viaduct was being constructed in the 1870s. Several narrow gauge lines were built across this area to transport the stone blocks and bricks required for the construction process.

With the slopes of Ingleborough in the distance, the building of Ribblehead Viaduct is well underway. The fascinating methods used to construct the arches and piers are on view. Huge amounts of timber are being used as formers and scaffolding to enable the stone masons and brickies to put the whole viaduct together. Various huts are sprinkled around the site in front of the structure. These would form the buildings for the navvies to work in and also for the brick kiln on site and depot for the small locomotives used. A brick kiln was also in this area.

Engineers excavated below the undulating surface through the peat and clay to find solid rock for the foundations of the piers. They started the foundations and stone-work from the middle of the structure - it's documented that pier 13 was the first to rise from the ground in 1870. The engineer in charge, Mr Crossley, had not decided at the start how many arches there would be, but had to create the structure on a gentle curve of one mile radius and with an ruling gradient of no more than 1 in 100.

Steam operated cranes can be seen on the top of the arches which would be used to lift materials as the arches were built above the piers. The point where the arches form is termed as the 'spinging point'.

MIDLAND RAILWAY.
SETTLE & CARLISLE
(SETTLE TO HAWES JUNCTION)
& HAWES BRANCH
LAND PLAN.

Titles of Acts..

The colour photograph below shows a very similar view of the north eastern corner of the viaduct site to the one on the previous page, but some 125 years later. This is a picture taken during the extensive repairs of the mid 1990s. The area in the foreground can be compared to the 1870s view with all the construction huts and other works on this site.

A particularly fascinating and rare photograph of the 1870s site at Batty Green. The piers are beginning is rise out of the foundations below and the shanty town accommodating hundreds of navvies and engineers is on display in the background. This view was taken around 1872 as it is known that the piers at the southerly end began to form in the summer of that year. The 24-arched viaduct was built in stages of six piers at a time and from different starting points which allowed construction gangs to progress at the same time. The 'springing points' from which the arches were eventually formed, started to appear from the northerly end as the materials and equipment required were progressed by a temporary narrow track built from the embankment.

It was in 1869 that the first steps were taken here to develop the site for construction of the viaduct and tunnel at Blea Moor. The early engineers of the Midland Railway Company decided that temporary accommodation would have to be built near the site to house the men and their families. By July 1870 more than 40 huts had been erected. These huts offered three areas of accommodation, one for the main family, another for lodgers and a third area for a kitchen and dining area. A visitor in 1872 quoted, 'The hardy wives of railway operatives decorated their wooden walls with paper hangings and pictures cut from illustrated newspapers'.

Blea Moor

Tunnel Huts

Jerusalem

Jericho

Belgravia

ıkerman &
Sebastopol

Batty Green

Salt Lake

12

Shanty Life

The settlements that evolved in the 1870s, when the viaduct was under construction, were on a tract of moor-edge known as Batty Moss, part of the Ingleborough estate of the Farrer family. It had become known as Batty-wife-hole after a pothole filled in by the railway builders but still remembered when Batty's wife had drowned in a pool. Hereabouts were housed around 2,000 navvies, many with families. Apart from the Midland's yards and offices were public amenities – shops, a hospital, post office and eventually day and Sunday Schools.

Railway activity around Ribblehead sprang from the appearance of a tractor-hauled van. Ten men, including surveyors, who were to make experimental borings, lived in that van during the winter. The equipment needed for their survey was carried on the backs of donkeys. A writer in "Chambers's Journal recalled having to stand by the van for half an hour with the bull's eye as a guide to the men homecoming through the waste. Sometimes one would stick and his mates would have to dig him out. "There were two chain o' knee-deep water four times a day for the fellows atween their meat and their work."

Of the shanty towns, Batty Green – the largest – sprawled on the southern side of the Moss. Inkerman and Sebastopol were located close to the viaduct. To the north-east stood Belgravia, where presumably the better class of worker was housed.

Job Hirst, master mason and sub-contractor for Ribblehead Viaduct, arrived by train at Ingleton. He was an important man in the Ribblehead story. His hut was in a salubrious area beside the turnpike road and well away from the boggy area. As he stood at the door, the burgeoning viaduct was plainly visible. He had a short walk to work. Good wages were paid to the men but they jibbed at being exposed to bad weather. Masons risked being blown from the temporary decking by wind racing up Chapel-le-dale. Alas, Job had an unhappy ending. He died after being attacked and robbed by several men as he returned from business in Ingleton. His inscribed gravestone can be seen on the right after passing through the lych gate at Chapel-le-Dale church.

The construction of Ribblehead Viaduct was managed by Charles and Walter Hurst, who had a workforce of 60 Welsh masons, all of whom were skilled. A narrow gauge railway connected Batty Green with the viaduct and also with excavation work on the south side of Blea Moor tunnel. It was in 1870 that the ground was disturbed as the first few foundations of piers were sited. There was mossland as well as heather moorland.

The worst mosses lay on the Ingleton side. Their names were Gunner Fleet Moss and Low Moss, Parker's Moss and Bruntscar Moss. One of tasks was motivating the stonemasons who were dressing the blocks of stone taken from the ground at Whernside. The dressing was done by "plug and feather", a wedge driven into the stone and hammered until that stone broke.

A more modern day scene with a hippy encampment in 1988. It shows the area where navvies based themselves at Batty Green in the 1870s.

A contractor's hotel.

Built on Wool

Ribblehead Viaduct was said to have been built on wool. The Midland Railway Company, forever short of money to finance their grandiose plans in those inflationary times, may have borrowed money from the Woolmen of Bradford. About 100 men would be employed on the viaduct.

The viaduct was to have twenty-four arches, every sixth pier being of extra strength "so that if, from any unlooked for contingency, any one arch should ever fall, only five arches could follow." The first stone of this massive structure was laid by Mr William Ashwell on October 12, 1870. The last arch was turned in October, 1874.

Construction was completed from north to south, stone being found in sufficient quantities in Littledale, adjacent to Whernside. It was limestone taken from an especially low level of Whernside. Men had to dig down 25 feet to reach it. The eventual requirement was for 30,000 cubic yards of masonry. The mortar that bound stone to stone was mixed using a 10hp engine. Local lime was not considered suitable. The contractor favoured Barrow lime from Leicestershire.

Deep foundations were necessary. Men dug down to reach a bed of limestone that would give the piers the needed stability. Limestone, dressed by "plug and feather" formed the masonry. It was acquired from the aforementioned two quarries under Whernside. They lay at a distance of one and a-quarter miles. Stone was transported to the site of the viaduct by locomotive.

Batty Green had its own brickworks, managed by Robert Nixon, who had the assistance of his brother John and twenty-eight workers. The Nixons were suited to their work. They hailed from Northampton, which was good brick-making country. The arches of the viaduct would absorb one and a-half million bricks.

Only six arches were turned at a time, lessening the need for a vast amount of timbering. As the piers emerged from deep in the ground, they were timbered to enable a steam crane to operate. The piers have a sure foundation.

Varied Activity

At the foot of the viaduct was a network of tramways, passing round the steepest of curves and on inclines as steep as 1 in 18. Also existing were mortar mills, brick-making machines, drying sheds and kilns. A ten-horse power engine was constantly in use for mixing mortar. The requirement was for 30,000 cubic yards of masonry and 3,000 cubic yards of concrete.

Black marble, for the masonry, was dug out of a quarry on the Ingleborough Estate. A steam crane was employed to unload the stone. Two hand cranes and their travellers turned the stone and settled it in place. Batty Green was provided with its own brickworks. Half a million bricks went into several layers to form the arches. The crown of each arch would be covered in a light concrete -type mix before an early type of pitch was used over that to create a waterproofing effect. The internal aspects of the viaduct below the rails are intriguing. Voids are created between the arch structures and at the top were covered with 8-inch thick 'Horton' flag stones to give cover and strength before the ballast and track was placed on top.

Map showing the parcel of land acquired from the Farrer family to build the line of railway and viaduct.

The brick-making establishment at Batty Green, under the management of Mr Rixon, covered a large tract of moorland, having drying sheds, ovens, a large patent brick-making machine by Porter and Co, of Carlisle, a crushing machine and a traveller seventy yards long to deliver the bricks in the shed above the ovens where they were dried by waste heat.

There were ten ovens, each holding from 14,000 to 15,000 bricks. Twenty thousand bricks a day were produced. The glacial clay on the moss was found to be free from limestone pebbles that would have caused the bricks to shatter under the heat of the kiln. Incidentally, the wife of the brickworks manager ran away with a local navvy. A pursuing policeman lost sight of them at Skipton.

Mr Ashwell, the contractor, did much to make the workmen comfortable. The men who were on the gantry had boxes to shelter them from the weather. At ground level, the masons had sheds for comfort. Many of the masons were paid 6s.6d a day. Others worked nine hours a day for only 6s.3d. In summer, the contractor required them to work for ten hours a day, paying an extra 8d per hour. In March, 1872, there was a strike of masons. They were demanding more money. The outcome is not known but presumably they returned to work fairly soon with extra cash.

The number of arches could vary between 18 and 24, John Crossley, Midland engineer, favoured 24 arches and this was approved by the Midland's construction committee. The work was attended by a number of impeding problems – the hardness of the stone, the flooding of quarries by the beck and the general wetness of the moor.

By 1873 the first twelve piers of the viaduct were arched. In due course, when the work was complete, the handsome structure was topped off by parapets of gritstone. The engineers proudly told their friends that when each wooden frame was removed from an arch, it dropped a mere quarter of an inch. Stone from a quarry in the vicinity of Salt Lake was heaped between the Ingleton road and the viaduct as a mighty embankment holding 200,000 cubic yards of material.

A contemporary drawing of a viaduct under construction on the Settle-Carlisle line. It is possible to see some of the techniques used to prepare the wooden formers and scaffolding to enable the stone piers and arches to be erected.

Name.	Abode.	When buried.	Age.	By whom the Ceremony was performed.
William Dean No. 233.	Sebastopool	Jan. 22	11 months	Wm Harper
John Hollenshaw No. 234.	Sebastopool	Jan 24	40 years	Wm Harper
Charles Bibby No. 235.	Sebastopool	Jan. 31	9 months	Wm Harper
Louisa Annie Thompson N. 236.	Jericho	Feb. 1	3 years	Wm Harper
Fredrick Little No. 237.	Inkerman	Feb. 5	4 years	Wm Harper
Tom Atkinson Little No. 238.	Inkerman	Feb. 9	1 year & six months	Wm Harper
Thomas Smith No. 239.	Jericho	Feb. 12	10 months	Wm Harper

BURIALS in the Parish of Chapel le Dale or Ingleton Fells in the County of York in the Year 1871

Life at Batty Green

Wooden huts to accommodate the workers were of standard size. When constructed, the roofs were covered with boiling tar. Each hut had three rooms – one for the hut-keeper, another for general activities and the third for lodgers. Uninvited guests were – rats! A religious life was available. James Tiplady, of the Bradford Town Mission, commenced his ministry at Batty Green in the June of 1870. William Fletcher ran a mission further north. Burials took place at St Leonard's Church, Chapel-le-Dale. As the years went by the churchyard had to be extended.

There is a popular idea that the Settle-Carlisle railway was built by navvies, when in fact over a score of specialist skills were needed. Masons were needed for stone and brickwork. Some stones weighed eight tons. Carpenters prepared the timber framing that would enmesh the emerging piers until, with the arches turned, the framing could be moved on, to be used for another set of piers.

An inkling of life in a shanty hut was given in an article that appeared in Chambers's Journal on March 8, 1873. A navvy did not keep fashionable hours. He was described as "a very rough diamond; but when you come to mix with him familiarly, and to understand him, you come to realise that he is a diamond.." An engineer admitted that the English navvy has his bad points, almost all his troubles being the ale-can. "But with these bad points there are many elements of the true pith and ring of the English character."

Strange stories were told of Chapel-le-dale. The men who built the viaduct were familiar with the church at Chapel-le-Dale, having attended funerals of friends who had been lost to railway work. Hurtle Pot, behind the little Chapel, was said to be the haunt of a boggle which lured visitors to their doom in a deep pool, which was said to be inhabited by black trout. When weird strains were heard by a courting couple passing on the nearby track, they scurried away. Eventually, from Hurtle Pot, a man emerged. He had been practising playing the violin.

A page from the burial register at Chapel-le-Dale church. Names of some of those who died at Batty Green during the construction period are accompanied by their 'abode'. Places such as Sebastopol and Inkerman were familiar names from the Crimean War period when railway navvies built lines up to the front line.

18

Maintenance

Rain, not the notorious wind, caused the major damage to Ribblehead Viaduct. The drainage system involved hollow spandrels – those triangular pieces at the head of the piers – and iron downspouts. As time went by, water seeped through in the wrong places – cracks in slate and layers of asphalt that had deteriorated. The viaduct looked like an ailing giant in "splints".

One of the slabs of slate – actually the local type, known as Horton flags – was removed and a manhole cover fitted to enable men to explore and examine the spandrel-voids. That "black limestone" of Littondale, of which the viaduct was built, came to be regarded as "bastard limestone". When an engineer used this term he was not swearing. He was simply commenting on its nature.

When I visited Ribblehead Viaduct in January, 1983, I saw it at close quarters. It looked awesome – and careworn. The viaduct was being attended to, like a patient being subjected to a series of major operations. Once a week, an official from the works department had arrived at Ribblehead to check on the patient's health. It was done with the aid of binoculars.

Every hole and crack was clearly visible. Over £500,000 had been spent on repairs since 1970. Some of the piers stood ankle deep in old bricks, long since replaced. Some of the piers were reinforced with old railway lines set vertically against the grey stones and firmly braced. Other ingenious ways had been devised to off-set the ravages of time and the weather.

The permanent way was laid throughout with 82lb steel rails and was adapted for heavy traffic moving at high speed. Harry Cox, of Settle, provided me with lots of fine detail about life when working on a viaduct like Ribblehead. He was 92 years of age when we chatted a length in 1976. His memory stretched back to a time when workmen wore rough shirts and fustian trousers that were tied below the knee with a york [a strip with a buckle that allowed the knee and leg freedom of movement]. Most men wore caps. Inspectors donned bowler hats, this being part of their uniform.

Left: **The large scale of Ribblehead Viaduct presented structural engineers with a headache. The piers stetching some 104 feet above Batty Moss had to have scaffolding erected before any repair work could begin. The repairs in this photograph were carried out in the summer 1990.**

Above: **With the end of steam in the North West in the summer of 1968, diesel locomotives appeared on all services. This train heads south at Ribblehead with a Class 45 diesel locomotive. These through services continued until the early 1980s when they eventually were re-routed away from the line. The railway had already lost its local services in 1970 with only Settle and Appleby stations still open for business for an occasional service from Leeds to Carlisle.**

Right: **A patch repair to one of the giant piers holding up the viaduct. Old rails were strapped around the stone pier to help prevent it splitting away.**

Below: **This photograph shows the extent of the problem exacerbated by rain and frost over the years. Large cracks developed between the brick arch and stone faced voussoir which would require repair.**

While working on the viaduct, long years ago, Harry Cox and the other men had to often face strong winds from the west. Said Harry: "These winds came racing up Chapel-le-Dale. The arches seemed to suck them through. Work on the masonry had to stop and every small item – tools, etc – either removed from the scaffolding or secured firmly.

Harry remembered a goods train passing. The door of a van must not have been properly secured. It blew open. "Lots of boxes containing kippers came flying out. We should have collected the boxes and taken them to the station. Some of them were delivered but we also managed to live off kippers for weeks!"

Work on the viaducts in t'owd days was not easy. Eventually, scaffolding came in small lengths that were bolted together. "We had to use a crab [hand-operated winch] to draw up lengths of scaffolding a hundred feet long." There'd be one cabin per length and one near each large viaduct or tunnel.

The Ribblehead cabin, standing on the embankment to the north of the viaduct, was entirely home-made from such material as railway sleepers. Workmen made their own seats. The foreman knocked up a rough cupboard in which he could keep his stationery. At leisure times, clay pipes were popular. They were packed with black twist at threepence an ounce. Harry Cox smoked 4 oz a week when it was at that price. "You were someone in those days if you smoked using a wooden pipe... There was also a lot of tobacco-chewing -and spitting."

Several summers were spent re-bricking under the arches of Ribblehead viaduct. The first task was to fit "cat heads. These were wedged under rails, and extended, with two bends to overhang the parapet and, using ropes and blocks, made it easily possible to raise heavy baulks of timber. Scaffolding poles were erected around the piers, ten to each pier. At about 80 ft long, the poles reached to just beyond the head of the piers.

When re-bricking, two arches were attended to at the same time. Harry Cox's boss during this operation was Jackie Smith, from Carleton. The operation depended entirely on him, for there was no inspection to check that the work had been correctly carried out.

When two arches had been re-bricked, all the timber was lowered to the ground with the "crabs" and moved by improvised tramway to the next arches. The bricks used for the arches were Staffordshire [blue bricks]. Mr Cox helped to re-brick all the arches, a task that took two or three summers. "In amonghands, in winter, we worked in Blea Moor Tunnel."

Right: **It was the water and wintry conditions at Ribblehead that caused the viaduct to deteriorate rapidly.**

Below: **Scaffolding around some of the arches ready for repair work. Pier No.7, in the distance, required more work than the others.**

Blea Moor Tunnel

Linked to the construction works at the viaduct in the 1870s was the building of a tunnel under Blea Moor. This, the longest tunnel on the line, was 2,629 yards long and took five years to build. Seven shafts were sunk up to 500 feet below the Moor to enable 16 separate work faces to proceed in the tunnelling work. Often working by candlelight, up to 300 miners, bricklayers and labourers worked on the project which ran simultaneously alongside the construction of the viaduct.

The use of the recently discovered substance Dynamite was used extensively to blast away the rock which was then hoisted up the shafts to be deposited in areas on the Moor.

Above: **As well as gaining access for workmen to the face of the tunnel works, much of the spoil extracted from the mining was lifted up through the shafts. This one was converted into a vent to allow smoke to escape from the tunnel below. The Yorkshire peak Ingleborough is dominating the distance.**

Left: **The southern portal of Blea Moor Tunnel. Mounds of spoil from the tunnel can be seen littered on the tops. The curvature of the line as it turns to the right can be followed by the piles of the extracted rock.**

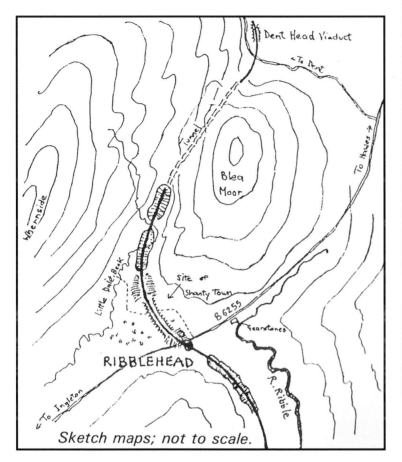

Left: **This picture shows the tunnel mouth at the southern end and the distant signal that was positioned there until removed for display at Settle station close to the preserved signal box. The dilapidated Masons' pattern platelayers hut is seen in front of the tunnel mouth on the right.**

Top right: **Looking down from Blea Moor northwards towards Dent Head. This tunnel vent is the most northerly of those remaining.**

Right: **A unique view right down into one of the tunnel shafts. A possession of the line was in place and workmen can be seen on the trackside during a maintenance period.**

Left: **The northern portal of Blea Moor Tunnel.**

Above: **A very different landscape is on view as the railway leaves the northern end of the Tunnel. The line ahead is reaching towards Dent Station, the highest main line station in England. The viaduct in view is Dent Head which itself has received a major series of repair works in recent times. The forestation in this whole area has been relatively recent, with the conifers grown mainly for wood pulp.**

Previous page: **A steam special bursts out of Blea Moor Tunnel heading for Dent.**

Above left: **A moorland sheep appears to conquer one of the spoil heaps on Blea Moor.**

Left: **Just to the south of Blea Moor Tunnel is this aqueduct which carries Force Gill down from the sides of Whernside and over the railway.**

Above: **A picture looking south of the cottages, water tank and signal box at Blea Moor in steam days. Most of the cottages have now gone as has the water tank, but one house remains with the signal box close by. Steam locomotives would often use the water tower here to replenish their tenders ready for the next stage up the 'Long Drag'.**

Opposite page: **The lonely house at Blea Moor in the 1990s. One of the three Yorkshire Peaks, Ingleborough, stands proudly over the whole scene.**

Blea Moor Signal Box

Above: **The remoteness of Blea Moor signal box left the signalman a good hyke from the main Ingleton to Hawes road and up past the viaduct.**

Top right: **An up 'home' starting signal controlling one of the sidings at Blea Moor.**

Right: **Blea Moor signal box is an LMS-style structure which replaced an earlier Midland design in 1941. The Settle-Carlisle line is one of many railways being upgraded to colour-light signalling and so in the years to come, this box and others along the route will become redundant.**

The 1892-built signal box which was sited on the down side opposite the railway cottages. In a remodelling exercise in 1941 which saw the sidings increased into loop lines, this was demolished and the new signal box built on the up side (pictured on the previous page).

Winter on the Railway

Above: **Almost buried under snow drifts, Ribblehead station is often battered by storms in the winter. This particular year closed the line for several days in the harsh winter of 1947.**

Right: **A train waits in the down loop opposite Blea Moor signal box. The signalman is discussing the line conditions with the driver of the diesel locomotive.**

Previous page: **Signalling instruments from Blea Moor signal box.**

Life at Blea Moor following a very heavy snow fall. The snow plough has been brought into use to help clear the railway. The signal box and water tank are plastered in snow.

Ribblehead is in direct line with weather coming in from Morecambe Bay to the west. In winter, the area which is 1030 feet above sea level, can get ice and snow which turns the landscape into a completely different place. The winter of 1947 saw the line cut off to traffic for weeks when drifting snow took hard-pressed gangs some eight weeks to re-open the railway. In 1963 similar conditions prevailed and no regular trains passed through for five days. A south-bound express got stuck in a drift near Dent and had to be dug out with some carriages returning to Carlisle.

From the footplate of a short north-bound goods train carrying coal, the area around Blea Moor is seen to good effect. The signal box, water tower and loop lines are clearly visible. This section of the Settle-Carlisle was remodelled in 1941 to increase capacity for train movements.

A Class 60 diesel locomotive hauls a heavy train load of gypsum towards Blea Moor on its journey to the works at Kirby Thore.
Inset top left: The final Stationmaster at Ribblehead, Bill Sharpe and his son Geoffrey who was a porter. Bill would send weather information to the Air Ministry and, *right inset*, a balloon was used to measure some weather conditions.

An icy cold Ribblehead Station and Whernside dominating the background. When local services stopped using the line in 1970, the smaller stations started to fall into disrepair. Ribblehead was very open to the elements and quickly deteriorated. This scene looking north shows the siding to the left which served the limestone quarry. By the early 1990s things started to look up - the new down platform was built and trains started to call into Ribblehead both ways once more.

Ribblehead Station

Following years of neglect, the station at Ribblehead was completely refurbished from a derelict building into a new visitors' centre. Owned by Network Rail and now managed by the Settle-Carlisle Railway Trust, many thousands of pounds were raised from national and local organisation to fund the works. The Friends of Settle-Carlisle Line and The Railway Heritage Trust were among the prime funders.

After the Settle-Carlisle was saved from closure in 1989, it was a matter of rebuilding train services and stations to their former glory. Ribblehead station was closed in 1970 as part of the cutbacks at the time and the down platform and buildings were demolished.

As part of the regeneration period, a new platform and waiting shelter was constructed and located this time to the south of the main station buildings. This allowed access to the siding which is now used for loading various commodities including timber. This view is looking south towards the 1994-built platform.

The refurbished station buildings at Ribblehead are picked out nicely in sunshine as Whernside is shrouded in low cloud.

As part of the general upgrading of stations along the line including here, newly installed gas-type lamps have been erected to finish off the heritage-style of the ex-Midland Railway stations.

The station at Ribblehead had a complete rebuild, including new windows, a new roof and barge boards. The interior has been fitted out as an exhibition hall and shop and is open to the public most of the spring and summer under the auspices of the Settle-Carlisle Railway Trust.

Stop
Look
Listen
Beware
of trains

Way out →

Left: **Before the structure was rebuilt, passengers had no facilities at Ribblehead to protect them in bad weather. This 'passenger' had suffered particularly badly by the look of it!** *Above:* **Ribblehead's 24 arches required 24-hour attention during the renovation process.**

Re-birth of Ribblehead Viaduct

The year of 1989 was the key date which signalled the re-birth of the Settle-Carlisle Railway. The prime structure to receive attention was the viaduct at Ribblehead which it was estimated by British Rail was to cost £6m in repairs. This figure was hotly disputed by many during the campaign period to save the line. More realistic figures were produced which put repair costs at a third of the original one. Trial repairs were carried out on several piers and arches out of the 24 on the viaduct just to prove that stone and brick replacement work could be achieved at a fraction of the cost.

A key letter sent from the Transport Minister Paul Channon to local Lancaster MP Dame Elaine Kellett-Bowman announcing that the Settle-Carlisle line was to be reprieved. Following many years of campaigning by many local and national groups, most notably The Friends of the Settle-Carlisle Line and a petition which was signed by 30,000 people, the railway was safe and after trial repairs to Ribblehead Viaduct carried out in the summer of 1988 proved, the whole structure could be repaired at a fraction of the well-publicised £6m.

A document detailing the trial repairs to 'Bridge No. 66 Ribblehead Viaduct', outlined proposed work on King Pier No. 12 and No. 13 and associated arches. A waterproof membrane was also fitted over the area of these two arches. The contact was let to GKN Colcrete Ltd., who began working on 25th July 1988 for a 13-week period. This successful trial repair to two arches became part of the bid to save the line from closure which came just a few months after the repairs were completed.

DEPARTMENT OF TRANSPORT
2 MARSHAM STREET   LONDON SW1P 3EB
01 276 3000

My ref:

Your ref:

Dame Elaine Kellett-Bowman DBE MA MP
House of Commons
LONDON
SW1A OAA

11 April 1989

I have decided to refuse consent for British Rail to close the Settle-Carlisle railway line. I enclose the text of a Statement I am making to Parliament today.

I very much hope that the organisations and individuals who have fought strongly for the retention of the line will now give it their practical support.

PAUL CHANNON

Two of several alternative plans put forward by British Rail architects in case the existing viaduct could not be repaired.

From the days of the line being threatened with closure in 1983, BR even considered selling off the line as a private enterprise to the highest bidder. Without the secure knowledge of Ribblehead viaduct being of a sound nature, this became almost impossible and initially a scheme was devised to take up the single line of track and ballast and lay down a membrane to protect the deck from water ingress. This process was considered to be one of the most important aspects to the viaduct's restoration. The work was carried out in October 1989 during a general possession of the line. Over 40 men worked in three shifts to get the £400,000 contract completed.

Above: **This graphically shows the extent of the problems facing Resident Engineer Tony Freschini and his team.**

Left: **With excavators and cranes in attendance, the ballast was removed from the viaduct floor in October 1989 ready for a new waterproof membrane.**

An Ailing Giant

The period of Ribblehead Viaduct's most rapid decline was from the 1950s to the 1980s. The last steam train under the old regime used the Drag on August 11, 1968. Henceforth, we saw faceless diesel locomotives.

Half a million pounds were spent on Ribblehead viaduct during the 1970s. For two weeks, in the autumn of 1989, the line was closed as Ribblehead Viaduct had its deck waterproofed. Before any work could be started, the rails were lifted and 2,500 tonnes of ballast removed. At the same time the parapet walls were strengthened with concrete, which in addition to providing a clean line to work to, enabled the waterproof membrane to be keyed in, giving a total seal.

Next came the laying of the waterproof membrane, a layer of Wolfin IB on "Terrafix", which is not unlike thick carpet felt. Another layer of "Terrafix" was placed on top, protecting the membrane from damage by the ballast, which was then replaced and the track re-laid. Powerful arc lights enabled men to work in shifts throughout 24 hours.

Ribblehead Viaduct looked like an ailing giant in splints. Individual stones had been secured using bolts and cartridges. The latter, made of mortar in a plastic skin, were known to the railway workers as "sausages". I studied a block of limestone that had fallen some 70 feet from he top of a pier. The friable nature could be seen in a hundred places. There was cracking and "shelling", each an invitation to the frost to penetrate and cause further damage.

A 30 mile an hour speed restriction came into force. Early in 1981, a report indicated that Ribblehead Viaduct was deteriorating to such an extent that it would either have to be replaced within as little as five years or the line would be closed. The figure of £6m was mentioned.

Rain, not the notorious wind, was causing the major damage. The rainfall averaged 70 inches a year, though in 1954 the total was over 100 inches, five of which felon a single December day. The century-old drainage system involved hollow spandrels – those triangular pieces at the head of the piers – and iron downspouts. Water seeped in the wrong places, through cracks in slate and layers of asphalt that had deteriorated.

After finding its way into the heads of the piers mixed with the "fill" – the mortar and rubble – reducing this to a sort of clayey mud. The water eventually trickled through the outer skin from dozens of cracks between the squared limestone, having washed away the mortar. Lime used for the original mortar was "hydraulic", brought from Barrow near Leicester. The mixture with local sand had not been satisfactory. By the early 1980s, it might be raked out when dry and washed away by escaping water during periods of heavy rain.

The men with whom I chatted during the most recent restoration hailed from Lancashire. One of them, who was engaged in brickwork – durable red bricks, of the Accrington type – pointed to a six-inch diameter hole and remarked that lile birds [blue tits] were roosting in it. It was mentioned to me that the blue-black variety of brick had first been considered but such bricks were not as suited to Ribblehead conditions as were those that were red

Stonework on the piers was replaced in a novel way. A cracked and battered stone was replaced by durable metal framework, with a mould resembling in its form the outer side of a stone. The gap behind was filled with tinted mortar, the men having in mind what tinge would be seen in years to come.

Previous page: **The entire viaduct as the contract to waterproof the decking proceeds. The old ballast was thrown over the side by diggers. The two piers at the centre of the trial repair in 1988 are clearly seen in the middle of the photograph following their restoration. Bags of waterproofing material are in view at the bottom right. Temporary concrete repairs to the structure can also be seen.**

The viaduct was often repaired in previous times as the weather and heavy traffic over the line took its tole. The brick arches would often need repairing and there are accounts of workmen carrying out these tasks in the early 20th century and over several summers. Wooden scaffolding and platforms would be erected.

Very little in the way of major repair work had been carried out latterly as freight and passenger train useage dropped off from the mid-1970s. The time had come to put the Settle-Carlisle line back into good order.

Right: **Work being carried out to the viaduct following reprieve from closure attracted great attention. Here, members of the press attend to view the ballast being removed before waterproofing could begin. Gradually the deck of the viaduct was being revealed with the tops of the arches beginning to show.**

The double-track line was reduced to a single line some years before to reduce the stresses on the structure. You can see the curvature of the viaduct as the line heads northwards. Also the bulk of

This page: **The undulating deck of the viaduct is created by the tops of the arches. Work progresses to repair the top of the structure ready for the plastic membrane covering. On top of that would rest the ballast and single line of track.**

Opposite page: **Pilot, Steve Harris, took this view of the viaduct and its surroundings. It is possible to see some of the narrow gauge lines of trackbed used by the 1870s engineers to cart materials around the site.**

The main waterproofing process is well underway here in late 1989. With heat-sealed joints, the main plastic waterproof sheet was protected both underneath and on top by another layer of material. This would help protect the plastic from being penetrated by ballast and other objects. New concrete haunches were built against the inner parapets which gave extra strength and a point to which the membrane could be attached.

A double celebration could be held in 1989 with the reprieve of the line from closure in the April and the viaduct's waterproofing in the October which would see the way ahead for the structure's long-term security.

This ingenious piece of machinery was brought in to inspect the viaduct. It allowed engineers to get a closer look at the stonework and other aspects of the structure and make a better judgment as to future repairs.

As soon as the line's reprieve came through and the test repair and waterproofing had taken place, it was time to look at the remaining 22 piers and their arches. £380,000 had been spent on the trial repairs and an anticipated further £2.7M required to complete the whole undertaking. By the end of 1989 the General Manager of the London Midland Region asked his staff to prepare drawings and procedures and the necessary contract documents.

Work began on site in July 1990 under contract holders Morrison Shand Construction.

Following the government's decision to reverse BR's wish to close the line, a minister with the Department of Transport, Michael Portillo, made a visit to Ribblehead. Primarily he was there to discuss a new 'down' platform at the station, but he also continued to the viaduct site to meet Resident Engineer Tony Freschini - on the right.

Above: Tony Freschini discusses findings with members of press at the start of the project. Once the ballast had been removed, it allowed sight of the deck above the arches. A hole in this view was discovered which once had an original wooden post from the building period within it.

Right: British Rail's construction teams also became involved in the main repair contract. Here, a group of employees are assembled who were mostly involved in the brick arch repairs.

Men employed by the main contractor's Morrison Shand pose in front of their handy work. The pier with scaffolding round it was isolated from the remainder of the project as it required more work to its stone block replacement than the others.

Scaffolding soon started to spread over the viaduct's arches and piers. Some 150,000 feet of scaffold was used. The project started from the southern end of the viaduct in the summer of 1990 and was due for completion in November 1991.

Working platforms were constructed on the scaffolding to allow contractors access to the stonework and arches. The main tasks were to replace cracked stones and re-grout the masonry joints. Over 200 holes were drilled into each pier with varying amounts of grouting, depending on the condition of each pier. This would be from 9 tons to 50 tons. Each King pier consumed some 300 tons of grouting in the voids within.

Right: **An indication as to the condition of much of the stonework. The cracking on this masonry would require the replacement of the stones with concrete replicas.**

Left: **Masonry being drilled out ready for props to be inserted to protect the integrity of the whole pier.**

Below: **Three props were used here which would remain in place when the concrete was poured in with shuttering surrounding the void.**

Above: **One of the piers also had this temporary concrete repair in previous times. These were all replaced by fresh concrete blocks.**

Left: **Members of the gang who used water powered tools to drill holes for grouting.**

Left: A closeup of an area where a cracked stone was once sited. You can see behind the props the original sand infill with rubble which was poured into the pier voids in the 1870s.

Above: Drilling one of the many holes into the masonry ready for grouting.

Top left: **Another damaged corner stone has been taken out, again clearly showing the sand filling tipped into the piers when constructed. The support props were inserted to protect the other masonry surrounding it.**

Left: **Re-inforcing mesh has been inserted into this corner stone ready for the new concrete mix which will form a replica of the original.**

Above: **A range of fibreglass shuttering was produced to re-create as near as possible an outer wall of the original block. As the description says, this was for Pier 4. Piers 7, 8, 9 and 11 were found to be in the worst state with pier 7 requiring 40 cracked blocks replaced.**

Above: **One of the most difficult blocks to replace were those forming the stone arch (voussoir). The tricky operation to take out and prepare shuttering for the new concrete can be seen.**
Below: **Job done, the newly cast concrete block.**
Left: **Newly cast concrete blocks are seen. These were deliberately coloured to blend in with the other masonry during weathering.**

Above: **We are now under one of the arches where an area of brickwork clearly needs replacing. Several layers of bricks were placed during the construction of the viaduct and subsequent repairs. A pile of new bricks are ready for inserting into the patch.**

Right: **Another view under one of the arches shows where the stone voussoir meets the line of brick. Bricks were made on site during the 1870s for the construction. The scaffold and working platforms were moved along the viaduct as work progressed.**

Top left: **A diamond core drill is being used to anchor the voussoir. This was one of the first piers to be restored.**

Above: **This view shows the work ahead of the engineers in repairing many aspects of the viaduct's construction.**

Left: **Timber was used to support the patch repairs to the arch brickwork. This was a very delicate operation as the new layer of brick had to be firmly against the inner layer to avoid further deterioration.**

BR and contractors' site engineer managers with progress on the project advancing well.

During the whole process from the line being saved in April 1989 and the full restoration of the viaduct, British Rail had spent £850,00 from their limited budgets on repairs. In addition to this funds were promised by various organisations to make up the full £3M required.

English Heritage £1M
Settle-Carlisle Railway Trust £499,000
Railway Heritage Trust £300,000
Rural Development Commission
£100,000
Many local authorities and the Friends of Settle-Carlisle Line channelled their donations through the Settle-Carlisle Railway Trust

With the bleak-looking Yorkshire peak of Whernside behind, this contractor is prepared for the cold conditions some 100 feet above the Batty Moss area at Ribblehead.

The date stone on the centre King pier was picked out in gold leaf to finish the project off properly. You can see the pointing between the masonry blocks which in the event was carried out over the whole viaduct. Two spandrel ties are seen.

Epilogue

The cost of renovating Ribblehead Viaduct in the most recent times was around £3m – almost the cost of the Settle-Carlisle line when it was built in the 1870s. I had the pleasure, with permission, of clambering up ladders and walking along boarding, which brought me within touching distance of the masonry. I stood a foot or so from one of the high ledges and heard that seed-eating birds had occasionally settled there, some seeds leading to the appearance of clumps of strawberries.

The exterior of one block of stone at maximum height held fossils from living organisms in a sea millions of years ago. Ribblehead Viaduct was much older than I had imagined. This viaduct epitomises the spirit of the Settle-Carlisle railway. I have seen it hundreds of times. Each time, the view has been different from its predecessors. Limestone, especially when wet, takes on the tones round about. The pattern of light and shadow alters subtlety with the slow progression of the seasons. The viaduct is especially appealing when holding the reds of a winter sunset.

A Divisional Engineer, years ago, commented: "You have to take your hat off to the men who built Ribblehead viaduct. When you consider the primitive equipment they had, it is a fantastic piece of engineering work."

To celebrate the achievements of not only restoring Ribblehead viaduct to its former glory but also the £100M spent on the whole line by Network Rail, special access was allowed to take a guided walk across the viaduct. This was held on two occasions in 2007 and again in 2009 during a possession of the line.

Volunteers from the Friends of Settle-Carlisle Line and Network Rail employees meticulously planned the events over many months to ensure a success and achieve safety during the walks.

All funds generated by ticket sales were ploughed back into projects for the line and a good time was had by all. Several thousand people queued up to walk across in July 2007 and the views greeting them were spectacular.

The stationmasters' house was the centre of operations for the viaduct walk. Rooms were allotted for planning and registration of the volunteers. The all-imortant rolls and cakes were made ready for the hungry walkers!

The house was subsequently extensively refurbished into a holiday let by the Settle-Carlisle Railway Trust.

On the second walk in August 2009, during appalling weather, TV's Emmerdale star, Tom Lister cuts the ribbon allowing the walk to commence. ITV's local weatherman John Mitchell and Tony Freschini look on.

Acknowledgements

Grateful thanks are given to the photographers for the loan of their pictures and especially to Tony Freschini who has provided such rare and important material covering the restoration of the viaduct under his title of Resident Engineer between 1989 and 1991.

Photographs
Courtesy of Tony Freschini collection pages 48 to 77
Mark Harvey pages 4, 5, 7, right 22
Roger Hardingham pages 6,12,15,18,23, top 25, 26, 28, 29, 30, 31, 36, 37, 38, 42, 44, 46, 58, 80
Bob Swallow 24, lower 25, 33, 35
Steve Harris pages 53 and 78
W R Mitchell collection - remaining photographs

Ribblehead viaduct in all its slendour with the third highest Yorkshire peak, Pen-y-gent in the distance. The helicopter was delivering bags of stone for the repair of the path running alongside the viaduct on behalf of the Yorkshire Dales National Park.